A Guide to 2(

S. B. KERMODE is an author of
living in Dorset. He started his career as a teacher of the arts,
but also had a life long passion for music and song writing.
It was this desire, to write lyrics worthy of attention, that got
him interested in poetry. Over the past 8 years he has
committed himself to his writing.

His debut novel, *Incurable Malady (2023),* explores themes
of injustice, the narrative driven by a vigilante activist who
takes the law into his own hands.

Morality, compassion and injustice are themes that run
strong through his work, forcing the reader to question what
is deemed normal; to remove the blindfold; update their
prescription; and finally see things clearly: that we are in
charge of our destiny via the decisions we make. That the
revolution has to be found within before the world can be
filled with love.

Also by S. B. Kermode

Fiction

Incurable Malady

Coming Soon

The Pylon (A Novella)

S. B. KERMODE

A Guide to 20/20 Vision

First published 2023 by S. B. Kermode
and The Osmia Archive.

theosmiaarchive.wixsite.com/publishing
Follow S.B.Kermode on both Facebook
and Instagram.

ISBN - 978-1-7392501-1-9

For the millions who have no say.

Contents Page

The Blind Man's Sonnet.

Our tender eyes born oppose tempered truths—
   Swathe such tender organs, protect them young,
Leash them so they don't leave the fields of grass,
   Plant hedgerows high, deny what's in the barn.
Many years of song and play to follow.
Willing, happy—acceptable, normal.
   Nowt perverse here! Says he who guards the gate.
   Nowt weird there! In your glass and on your plate.
But youths not young smell shit beyond the bull,
And peepers peep when bandages do fall.
   Now eyes sharp like the blade of crimson red,
   And eyes quake with the cries of coming death—
If such truths be fine then why do I weep.
Swathe me whole—cut the cords of memory.

The Revolution Within.

We can never be more than minor notes
in this cascade of diminishing scale.
A minority revolting against the lack of revolve
in this artery that will never find heart.

We have lost orbit—we are flying through space
towards distant desolate planets.
The blood spewing from the veins
because we forgot about the nature of the body—
we forgot about nature.

To restore the wounds caused by many
with this needle and thread
is more than one's fingers can bear.
Will this chorus of minor chords evoke emotion
when we lack compassion.

Minority: a feeling I felt so easily
fighting the majority. A resolution takes many
that can see eye to eye—so look me in the eye
and tell me what matters. It takes community—
though we can't stand our neighbours,
there are walls and distance between us.

Political grenades can not be beaten with hammers,
but caught in nets before they land.
Birds will not sing to the beat of your war drum.

If you can not throw kindness or sympathy
beyond the electric fence then your morality
has boundaries—boundaries that prove
our values are no more than skin deep
when there's a world around us.

Sonnet for a Dying River.

Dismay when they upon the river float,
  Adding salt to a murky flowing wound—
But wounds heal not when scratched beyond the bone,
  And poison nails adorn the gouging hand.
No longer swim where once the people bathed;
  Cast line nor bait for all the fish are dead;
Drink nowt that flows 'til done the river saved—
  But done be long where gov'ning bodies slept.
A river ill is a land ill in kind, but
  Solutions fall beyond the weathered maze;
Disrupt the birth of ever flowing coin;
  Bare ill perversion of our cultural ways.
    Shit in the river, watch it float downstream:
    One toxin more to fill our plastic sea.

Nowhere to Call Home.

High in the clouds, Thor hammers down—
it is the last remaining sound.
Bright flashing lights will light the night
with a silhouette of our time.

Bricks and cars will line the ground,
no one around,
not even a sound.

Broken glass reflects the past,
of withered trees and dusty skies,
of shattered dreams
and filthy lies.

Nowhere to call home,
no hope,
no money,
no family,
no soul.
Those politicians that I despise,
say respect our decisions
and accept our lies.
Nowhere to call home.

Our vision of Earth is just a star.
They say forget the Earth
we're heading for Mars.
There's a spaceship waiting in your backyard.

There'll be rain when the storm comes,
and tears in your eye,
as the ship you've been waiting for
returns from the sky.

Nowhere to call home,
no hope,
no money,
no family,
no soul.
Those politicians that I despise,
say respect our decisions
and accept our lies.

Nowhere to call home.

From the Plane Window.

From the plane window
 the sky grows infinite in all directions.
Below, the ground bleeds
 from green to brown;
 from trees to sand;
 from fertile to infertile land.

From the plane window
 I want to see the world whilst I still can.
From the engine
 I ignore the stream of diesel gas.

Kids next to me—
 their second time abroad.
We swap seats—
 and they struggle to ignore
        the column of smoke rising
 on the horizon.

When we arrive,
 we cover ourselves in cream
 to protect the skin from burning.
Inside the air is cool,
 but outside the plants are wilting.

The airport close,
 the sky shakes
 with the sound of passing planes.
Above our heads,
 weaving invisible threads
 into a thickening carbon tapestry.

But I want to see the world
 whilst there's still things to see—
I've heard out there somewhere
 is the last remaining bee;

fragments of an eco-system;
a peak with some ice;
a field with green grass;
and all these things
will soon pass.

Flex.

As I pass through my allotted passage of time,
I am aware of the disintegration of my flexibility—body and
mind.

My skin no longer springs back to form smooth, radiant
surfaces,
and my mind no longer accepts the lies regurgitated.

My limbs no longer explore new possibilities,
but instead fall back on ingrained muscle memory.

For so long, I have read between the lines,
I can no longer believe there is nothing to hide.

Yoga, a sequence of exercises to repeat,
if it's flexibility you want to keep.

Release the mind, find the flexibility to break free.
Sow the seeds for new possibilities.

But today, when I leant forward to pour that bleach,
I felt a pull in my hamstring.

And with that feeling—a feeling of pain—
my actions suddenly seemed insane.

Is the cleanliness of my toilet seat
more important than life in the sea,

struggling to breathe,
disintegrating in vast clouds of manmade toxicity?

Seeds.

I plant a seed,
and tend to its needs.
I give it water,
and give it warmth.
Then sit back and wait,
for that seed to germinate.

In a couple of weeks,
on the surface we'll see,
that little seed,
bear its green head.

Now if politicians had seeds,
they've all been planting weeds.
They're unpopular,
they're untidy,
and often quite spiky.

But we can take those weeds,
and put them on the compost heap.
We'll plant something new,
that bears fruit and is good for you.
A future where nothing is wasted,
and what you grow is nice and tasty.

Now if seeds were ideas,
I have a good seed right here:
let's make the world green,
and only grow what we need.

Now anyone can grow seeds,
it's not just politicians and corporate greed.
So go out and get a pack,
plant a seed and sit back.

Watch it grow,
and feel some hope.
In a world where it is hard to cope,
a seed is all you need.
Plant it.

Milky Sonnet.

I, young, I saw that normal in the norm—
  Normal happy cows in fields of pasture.
Drinking white from that of a new calf born—
  Old Mc Donald, the lessons brought laughter.
Photo in the sun with big happy eyes—
  Grass greener than green, lies cleaner than clean.
Muted, the mother's cries, the calves' goodbyes—
  Behind the green curtain, things seen unseen.
Milk to be strong, like farmer milking bull,
  To place seed in womb, carry calf to crate—
Born to pelt, leather coat, or cut for veal.
  Happy stories tell, forbade tell it straight.
      Draw curtains. Lie to be free of the lies.
      Child play; sing moo moo here and there, don't cry.

CONSUMER CHOICE.

Backward.

The cut of succulent flesh
lowers from the salivating mouth to the plate,
is sliced into its neighbouring piece.
Like mother birds of prey,
the family regurgitates the fragments of meat
and chews them back together.
At the end of the meal
(which is the beginning),
nobody says grace; no ritual of thanks;
no ceremony with hallucinogens to meet the spirit
of this mere ingredient
to thank it for its sacrifice. Backwards,
the mother carries the full plates into the kitchen
and slurps the dish up to the ladle
and back into the hot pan.
Salt solidifies and rises up to her fingers.
Pepper fragments crack into whole corns.
Moist herbs become brittle and dry
on their passage back into the container
and put upon the shelf. Slowly,
the hot pan empties itself
as the knife kisses the chopping board
and the mother collects the pieces
and puts them in the fridge—
an onion, a pepper, chilli, tomatoes,
and the breast of a Chicken
which she has uncooked
from a safe state of consumption
so that it is now pink and translucent,
marinating in its own slime,
with only a small amount of discoloured blood.

The ingredients taken back to the shop,
refunded; placed neatly in the open fridge, bleeding

cold air into the heated environment,
awaiting the stockist to return them to the store;
placed in a lorry; returned; unpackaged from their plastics;
vegetables placed in the ground;
Chicken returned to the butchers.
All day, the cleaver slowly lowers down,
aggressively jerks up;
a knife scraping against breastbone;
joining the fibres; reconnecting the tendons.
Like a machine that glues the jigsaw back together,
the individual unrecognisable parts
start to form a picture; like a potter
moulding the form of a sculpture
in pink wet clay. A head, wings, feet
rise up, out of the waste bin,
and with a few more abrupt lifts of the cleaver,
rejoin the pink body on the chopping board.
Later, another man aggressively stabs
anaemically white feathers into the bird's
wrinkled, pimpled skin, then hangs
its limp dead body up with the other birds
ready to have the toxic gas sucked from its lungs.

As the gas starts to clear,
these bodies of flesh become animated with life.
As if by some miracle the dead were once living—
their tinny weak hearts pumping blood
around their petrified limbs.
If their souls weren't already broken
the sound waves of distress would diminish
back to their snipped beaks.
The trolley of hanging birds rolls back
to the factory of tin and concrete
with its smell of shit and piss,
and the birds are left to struggle for space
in a pit of festering disease,
to make it through a floor of thousands,

17

like refugees in a camp
struggling to make it to the food bank,
to regurgitate corn riddled with antibiotics
and feel their bodies waste away in a matter of weeks.
Eventually, they will be unborn under halogen lighting
into non existence where they can dream
of the joy and potential of life.

Forward.

In the dream,
the joy and potential of life didn't include:
not being able to move for lack of space;
standing and lying in faeces; having beaks clipped
so that neighbouring birds aren't peaked to death.
Bred for their ability to fatten up quickly on little food,
the birds grow faster than they can cope with.
Unrecognised by poultry men
who do not have eyes to oversee
tens of thousands of birds,
a Low Pathogenic Influenza spreads
in an environment perfect for the evolution
of a Higher Pathogenic Influenza.
Birds drop dead so frequently
of the poor "living conditions,"
the cause is not recognised immediately.
The fitting birds with swollen heads;
with infectious excretions,
hidden amongst the many.
Before a conclusion is drawn, waste matter
is removed and spread over neighbouring fields.
Blackbirds and Robins feast
on infected insects and worms; a heavy rainfall
carries the run-off into the river and sea.
Aquatic birds who have no way to avoid this contaminant
Drop dead in their thousands. A mutation,
deadlier than seen in years spreads
around the world in the currents, and on wing.

A zoo reports its captive penguins die
as a result of the virus. Because of infection,
over half of UKs "free-range" Turkeys are slaughtered,
or die of dis-ease. Their bodies scraped up with JCBs,
their feathers, which are infectious,
fluttering into the surrounding hedgerow;
the bodies incinerated.

People worry about their Christmas dinner,
but the early bird who catches the worm
places a carcass on the table
and the festive cheer continues.
The time between putting up lights
and removing them again,
2.3 million birds become infected and die,
or are culled for prevention.
The virus spreads to Foxes, Otters, the odd Human.
The virus continues mutating.
In the streets, an activist warns passers-by
of the devastation of factory farming;
how they are a breeding ground for the next pandemic.
"90% of UK poultry is factory farmed!"
A pedestrian shrugs
and walks off eating his Chicken sandwich.

Fox.

Does a fox shaped flame
only burn at day break,
having danced through shadows
shifting with the night,
avoiding the spotlight.
You stand bold as brass
on a brick red wall
surveying your kingdom:

your urban playground.

Having made the transition
across the borderlands;
having adapted your tread
for harder grounds;
your gut for
rancid foods found.
Having become a dying breed
that kept breeding:

raising cubs in the new world.

Survivor of the slaying hand:
hands granted with dominion.
Finger on the trigger, hammer
on the plate, blood
on the heath—the lambs are safe
                                until
the hands crave more blood, and
the gut needs to be filled.

On the lip of the wall, the
top of the terrace, you
stand and sway
against the odds.
Your chestnut eyes

reflect the earth,
your tail dipped in snow.

In the twilight hours,
before the day crawlers
emerge from slab houses,
you breathe your last
moment of freedom.

Before the blue eyes of
God's sky cast down
a siege of judgement—
before greedy hands grasp
cold steel to
pepper your guilt with slugs—

bask in the glory of achievement.
Let the fire burn
through the contours of your being.
Then retreat,

become the earth,

cradled by the mother.

Road Kill.

Identifying rubber pressed fur,
  skull shattered sections reduced to dust.
    Clumped and mangled,
  torn and matted.

Like a Chameleon impersonating six mil tread
  in concrete grey.
The rapid clouds of a time-lapse night and day.
    Dust to dust, feed the flies;
        the haunting stare
    from your dust encrusted eye.
A final expression,
  fading, like a sun bleached painting.

The central reservation
    haunted by the shadows of corpses.

A witness to your daily erosion—
    taken away, cell by cell,
        by vehicles in motion.
Did you live beyond six months?
  A statistical average for foxes and badgers.

Were you blinded by the lights?
  Frozen like a statue when the music stopped.
Crippled by your own survival mechanism:
    serotonin and adrenaline—
        insufficient weapons
            against your mechanical nemesis.

Were you conscious long enough
    to see the red lights
        disappear into the night?
An image repeated again and again,
    but never the same friend that left you for dead.

A different registration plate,
    a different child's white face—
a child that was counting red cars,
    but now counts the remains of fox and badger furs.

Neglected:
    no merge in turn, no police tape,
        no shovel in hand or stretcher ready,
            no parallel universe, no resuscitation,
        no life support, no life.

No criminal investigation, no jury—
    only one sentence: a death sentence,
        but no sentence of remembrance,
            just the evidence written on the white lines
        of the central reservation.

The Matrix.

Ideas in films can seem like fiction, or horror conjured from contorted minds that see through dark eyes—warped imaginations. Imagine, we say, if all that were true, and beings were really kept in caged confinement, connected to machines and drained of their resources, treated like batteries to power something bigger!

We look out our windows to check the world is real. We pinch ourselves. Where are the smoke and mirrors? When is the grand reveal? How do they keep it so well hidden?

Deep in the country, behind the prickly pine, a tin house hums like the engine of a car. An invisible cargo transported back and forth in long vehicles, travels further into the wilderness.

Meanwhile, city dwellers huddle like aphids on a branch. When visiting that illusory countryside, so stuck in their ways, policed by ants, they follow the paths, go through gates—the crunch of gravel underfoot a sign they are on the right tracks.

A lorry pulls up at a warehouse shrouded in mist, miles of fields and private road in its wake. It reverses to the sliding door, and as the door rattles, and coils with the tug of a chain, for a short moment the mysteries of tin houses escape in the form of sounds. Everything echoes. A beast among many cries out into an air that is always dusk; a sharp bolt; a thud; the rattle of more chains, and a *snik...*

The shutter door closes to the sound of a *drip, drip...* and the lorry drives off.

In the country, walkers marvel at the red evening sky, but shudder when a breeze leaves them cold. They wrap up in their down-filled Berghaus and follow the map. Sometimes the road is rocky, but their sturdy leather boots grip the path well.

In the woods, the mist feels permanent. Lorries pass on long roads but the driver's face is rarely seen. Along a river of inaccessibility, a tin house sat on a slab of concrete permeates the smell of ammonia. Steam rises from the corrugated roof. Even at night, no light escapes its windowless walls. Very little escapes. Very little is seen.

After an exhausting hike, a couple remove their boots, draw the curtains and take the weight off their feet. Hungry, they crack the shells of happily laid eggs into the heat of a frying pan. The happy picture, above the label Organic, cleanses the conscience, although they never saw any chickens roaming on the farm. Later, the female whinges her monthly period has arrived, and that men are lucky they don't have to deal with that shit.

That night, they watch a film where everyone is plugged into a giant machine. The machine feeds and protects their minds by subjecting them to an enforced coma. In the coma, everyone lives happily in a perpetual dream. Children play in the fields, and the sun shines everywhere, other than the pine woods, which is shrouded in mist, and is always dusk. The film ends with a glitch in the system, and somebody wakes up.

Honey.

We dress up like spacemen
on a hot sunny day; we
dismantle the alien spaceship
and observe their behaviour.
We stand above them like
giants; like unwelcome gods
from another world.

Place drone between thumb and
finger and squeeze abdomen
until genitals erupt out,
collect the semen, chuck drone
on pile of dead drones; place queen
in clamp, open genitals with
tweezers, inseminate. Clip the
queen's wings so she can't escape.
Sit back. Watch bees work day in,
day out. When ready, steal honey.

When doused with smoke, the colony
believing a fire is imminent starts
to consume the honey; they are
not docile, just busy collecting their
belongings before their house burns
down. Forgot to ask the health
connotations of subjecting bees to
known carcinogen.

Like in the film Aliens by Ridley Scott,
there is a chamber of cells where
the queen lays her eggs; in the bottom of
tiny hexagons curled larvae glisten
milky white. The cells are sealed,
and when ready, a new life eats itself
free into a world of toil. All their
hard work, a sacrifice to the gods.

The boss who keeps bees said, if he
finds a new queen bee during hive
inspection, he kills it so it can't leave
and take half the hive—because he
has that right: he is one of those
many unwelcome gods from another
world, alien even to my own.

The thick white canvas makes us
immune to their venom, unlike
bears and tribesmen in the wild who
understand that for every ounce of
sweetness comes a rain of hell's fire.

The honey bee is so efficient at collecting
pollen, it is a less efficient pollinator than
other bees—bumble bee, mining bee,
leaf cutter, masonry, tawny, slender
and brassy. With ability to out compete.
Like in all agriculture, larger colonies,
larger hives become a breeding ground
for pests and disease. Bees would survive
fine—without the gods—nesting in trees.

The amount of honey a reduced colony
needs to survive a winter leaves little
if nothing to take. Most cheap honey
contains more sugar solution than
nectar or pollen.

Some keepers expect nothing for their
time—the flowers planted in the wild
garden. Other keepers want to feel
a world in their hands, even if that means
they crush it.

For an Upbeat Friend.

I wanted to write a poem
about the fox
I shovelled to the side of my drive
one cold morning,
when running late for work.
My partner called the council
to come and collect,
to dispose of in a manner
I imagine lacked compassion;
it was that or let it fester.

I began to read my lines
to the ear of an up beat friend,
who, conveying, with a furrowed brow
"You should write something lighter!
You're so obsessed with death!"
I closed my book and listened
whilst she talked about the kids:
the party; the presents; their trip abroad;
and Pete's huge salary—

All the while, thinking about the fox,
still on the side of my drive;
wondering when the council would come;
wondering whether, it would've been better
digging a hole in the flower border,
burying it where it belonged.

"Are you alright?" she asked:
I hadn't commented on her new car,
or the photo on her phone
of a child surrounded by presents.
"Sorry, I was thinking about the fox!"
"Stop wallowing; cheer up! When next we meet,
I want you dancing to a light-hearted beat!"

So we parted ways.
I dived to the depths
of my murky lake
and stared at my heart
restrained to the bottom with rocks.
Was it time to let it float;
come up for air?
It seemed at home down there
with the minnows and catfish,
but I had been given my orders.

I released the chains
and released the rocks,
but my waterlogged heart went nowhere.
It took effort to swim it to the surface.
On dry ground it spluttered;
it struggled with light;
it stammered words like:
"Why?" And, "Don't force me!
I'm a sensitive soul!"
I felt empathy for that part of me,
but I yelled, "Cheer up!
Your time moping in the macabre is up."
Though I didn't believe it.

My heart looked heavy;
not like the balloons on the party stand,
floating mid air,
vibrant with colour.
So I returned from the store with helium,
fed my heart till it was big and shiny,
floating by a main artery.
Its voice no longer low or glum,
but high; though it complained—
in an adorable way,
like a child restricted from play.

So I marched round to my friends,
showed her my meaty red heart
floating on an artery string,
confident I had it sussed.
She said, recoiling, "That's bloody disgusting!"
Where once I was up now I'm deflated. I said,
"I feel this happy stuff is well overrated."
Crossing her arms, "Do you really find it that hard?"

On my way home
I saw a girl with a heart-shaped balloon—
it was silver.
I saw the fox, still on the side of my drive.
It looked lost without life;
taken by some speeding car no doubt.
I wanted to write about
its lifeless body;
how with each passing day
I'd watched its soul drift away;
and how my heart was bleeding,
though it pulled on the string,
filled with helium.

Enough was enough.
I got me some paint,
smothered my heart in silver,
then in varying shades,
wrote the word "happy!"
in bubble font on both sides.
I contorted my face into a grin,
forced my fingers into my cheeks,
pushed up to reveal my teeth—
I felt like the Joker, with bats in his closet.
But I looked the part,
so I marched and marched
with a limpish hop
to the door of my up beat friend.

My face hurt from the forced effort,
but my friend saw my shiny heart
floating up high—
you should have seen the glint in her eye—
"You've done it! You've only gone and
bloody done it!" I didn't think I had,
but if she believed me,
it meant happiness was skin deep,
because inside I was thinking
about the fox on the side of my drive.

She took my heart with gusto,
and we marched on to the park.
She hadn't noticed my limpy hop,
or the fact I was faking.
When we arrived she let my heart go
and it drifted high into the sky,
and at first I panicked,
but the further it drifted
the less I felt, until eventually
I felt nothing.

Now, when I get home
I say "Evening Mr Fox,
why the drawn face?"
It no longer bothers me
he's the silent type.

A Word on the Wind.

How I lived my life:
arrogant, uneducated,
unaware, brainwashed.
The day it clicked:
When the male chicks fell
into the meat machine. When
a spiral of pig pink flesh was
snipped from its pig pink host.
When the teeth were pulled
and the beaks were cut.
When a man put his lubed arm
in a cow's dry vagina. When
they carried the calf away kicking
and the mother cried out
for her newborn.

When I realised
I was wearing someone
else's skin, and lying
under feathers plucked
leaving an eider
red and raw—
We let the eider down.
When the milk turned sour.
When I saw the abuse
of power.
When the hens helped
me in the garden.
When I looked into eyes
just like mine. We
smelt the air, and listened
to God's word
carried on the wind,
and it wasn't kill,
it was friend.

Bad Actors and Comedians.

Politics, a theatre
of bad actors,
comedians.
To believe a word they utter—
they parade
no truth,
no reason.

Jekyll and Hyde,
agendas disguised.
The illusion: we need them
gov'ning our lives.
"They fear free will,"
the audience heckle.

Learning
to go way back,
before all this
consumer crap.
Back the way things used to be,
before the black smog
of industry.

The narrative,
greed and fear.
No way to disappear.
Beneath the spot light
you're accounted for—
stand in line,
respect the law.

Laws keep changing.
Our lives dictated.
Who should I vote this year?
I vote they fuck off, disappear.

This Mini Ice-Age.

Strange, this mini ice-age,
conditions frozen in a perfect state—
      enough water
        trapped
        in ice;
  not so much vital heat
      reflects back to the skies.

Sea levels rise
      when ice water melts.
  Life becomes hell
for animals dependant
        on restricted land.

 We could retreat
to mountain peaks,
      but oxygen thin,
    our lungs give in.

 Too much ice,
vital heat reflects back
     to the skies—
     mini ice-age becomes
     sinister,
        savage.

 Cooling
 self perpetuating,
     frostbite taking limbs.
Nothing grows
 metres beneath snow.
    To become Eskimos
hunting fish through
sea ice.

Living on a snowball,
  intense white
        blinding eyes.

A mini ice-age—
not too much,
not too little:
    the perfect conditions
    for sustaining existence.

An instant of human neglect,
a system turned on its head.
    The earth,
        robust,
the atmosphere circling its crust
            fragile.

A cocktail of chemical elements,
  oxygen,
      carbon,
      nitrogen,
a balance governed by oceans,
  plants,
      trees—
      storing excess carbon,
providing life-giving oxygen.

    But we humans
keep polluting those seas,
        burning trees.
We cracking the earth's crust
        find things that combust—
      precious oil,
          petroleum.

Liquid gold controls our lives,
   powers cars we drive,
   nylon on thighs,
plastic in sinks,
influences
   the way corporations think—
big money corporations
   controlling politicians.

Black syrup's an issue—
   process of combustion
   releasing excess carbon—
a greenhouse gas;
a blanket
   trapping heat.

Icebergs and glaciers melt.
 Around the equator
   heat becomes hell.
   Global warming!
 Sea levels rise,
the seriousness of our neglect
   sinks in.

Flood Zone.

They say the climate's changing,
as the water's raging
through my front door.
They say greenhouse gasses
are destroying the ozone,
as we try to escape the flood zone.

For years the message clear,
but people just couldn't hear,
but now we can see
on our streets, on TVs.

A matter of urgency—
still government fracks our national parks,
corporations charge a fortune for electric cars.
I'd embrace solar power,
but I'm broke on this minimum per hour.

Whilst water's knee deep in my home,
some countries, the ground's dry as bone,
and though reservoirs run low,
big business bottles the rest
to improve cash flow.

Once a story, now reality.
Life style to be reviewed—
necessity to overrule luxury.
Years ago scientists said it—
government, corporations don't give a shit,
so long as there's profit.

Fuck you government,
fuck you consumerist,
fuck you insurance company
taking my money
and giving nothing back,
as the water's running through my door.

Gaia.

There were rocks and trees
with eerie human qualities,
like frozen figures fossilised.

Skin tones seeping through
lichen covered greys. Screaming
faces engrained in ancient Oak.

Twisting vines that squeeze and
choke. Neck and wrists bound,
possessions found.

Nature's mimicry, or encapsulation?
The question in question. Looking
for reason, but confronted
with rejection.

Theories dissected
section by section,
but still I see your face...

Civilisation reduced to a sacred few—
but if only they knew
why they were chosen to continue.

A man alive is no longer the same man.
A child reborn into a world reformed.
An apocalyptic wasteland—
vines grow in the cracks,
buildings house crows and wolves.

Animals tread the face of history,
cocooned in concrete, the face
of destruction, the face of greed.

The cleansing continues.

.

Acknowledgements

Thank you to people like James Wildman and Ed Winters for providing the information needed to help make the decision to go vegan. Watching *The Food Matrix - 101 Reasons to Go Vegan* opened my eyes to the decisions I was making and their impact on a world bigger than myself. It taught me that I have values and that my heart is full of compassion and empathy. It taught me that the industry of animal agriculture uses practices that only belong in horror films. And after watching, I realised I could no longer support this industry, or continue with that way of life, no matter what my tastebuds craved or what culture presented as normal. The journey to veganism is both painful and beautiful. Painful because of the knowledge that animals are treated so horrendously and that many people don't care, or turn a blind eye, even when they know the truth, just so they can continue as normal when there is nothing normal about the industry we have created. Beautiful because it teaches you love. It teaches you that you have the power to stand up for your values and you have the power to make a change.

I want to thank my girlfriend Sally Blood for supporting me in everything I do, for attending poetry nights, reading my manuscripts and taking this journey with me. A big thank you to Margaret Lewis for proof reading and being such a wonderful neighbour. And I also want to thank all the friends in the world who have the strength and bravery to step forward and be counted. Here's to a kinder world.

Shout outs to Derek Simnett, Gaz Oakley and Rich Roll for showing that you can live healthily on a vegan diet and that vegan food is not boring. Plus the good vibes.

Peace.

Printed in Great Britain
by Amazon